STARTING CHESS

Harriet Castor

Edited by Rebecca Treays

Designed by Maria Wheatley and Rachel Wells

Illustrated by Norman Young

Photographs by Howard Allman

Consultants: Clive Felton and David Norwood

Series editor: Cheryl Evans

SCHOLASTIC INC.
New York Toronto London Auckland Sydney

Contents

About chess

Chess is one of the oldest board games in the world. It was first played thousands of years ago. The game is a battle between two armies, called White and Black.

This book explains the rules of chess, and shows you how to use your pieces. There are tips, too, on how to attack and how to defend.

Chess can be quite a tricky game to learn, because there is a lot to remember at first. As you go through the book, you may need to look back at things you have already learned. Things you can look up are written in **bold**. You will see at the bottom of each page where to find them.

There are puzzles throughout the book, so you can test yourself. The answers are found on pages 30-31.

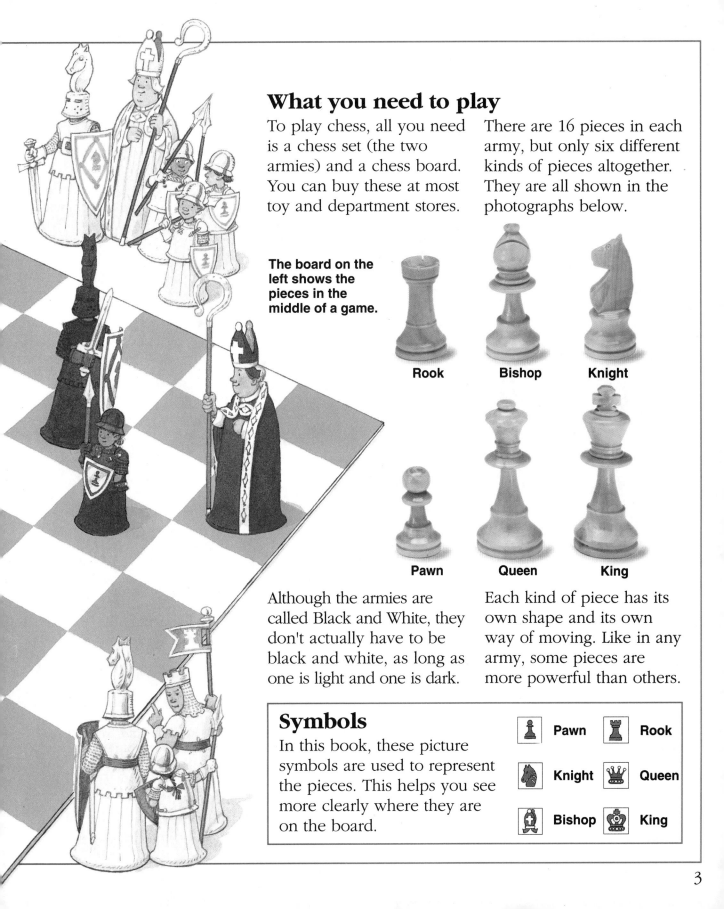

What you need to play

To play chess, all you need is a chess set (the two armies) and a chess board. You can buy these at most toy and department stores.

There are 16 pieces in each army, but only six different kinds of pieces altogether. They are all shown in the photographs below.

The board on the left shows the pieces in the middle of a game.

Rook

Bishop

Knight

Pawn

Queen

King

Although the armies are called Black and White, they don't actually have to be black and white, as long as one is light and one is dark.

Each kind of piece has its own shape and its own way of moving. Like in any army, some pieces are more powerful than others.

Symbols

In this book, these picture symbols are used to represent the pieces. This helps you see more clearly where they are on the board.

Pawn   Rook

Knight   Queen

Bishop   King

Setting up

At the start of a game of chess, the players face each other, with their armies lined up in front of them. The board is placed so there is a white square in the right-hand corner nearest each player. The pieces are always set out in the pattern shown below.

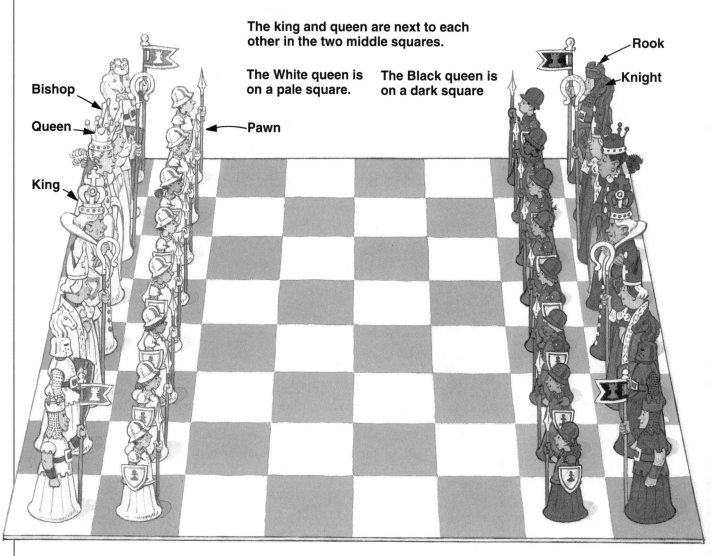

The king and queen are next to each other in the two middle squares.

The White queen is on a pale square.

The Black queen is on a dark square

Bishop

Queen

King

Pawn

Rook

Knight

The rooks are in the corner squares.

The knights are next to the rooks.

The bishops are next to the knights.

The pawns are in a row in front of the other pieces.

You and your opponent take turns at moving one piece each. But before you can play a full game, you have to learn how all the different pieces move and all the rules. It may seem difficult at first, but the more you play the easier it will get.

The board

A chess board is made up of 64 squares. The rows of squares across the board are called ranks.

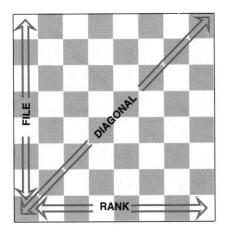

The rows up and down the board are called files. Lines of squares along a slant are called diagonals.

Arrows

Special red arrows are used on the boards to show where a piece is moving to, or when one piece is attacking another.

 This arrow shows a move. The arrow head points to the square the piece will reach at the end of its move.

 When one piece is attacking another, a dotted arrow points to the piece under attack. Remember, this is not showing an actual move.

Taking sides

The side of the board the kings are on is called the kingside. The side the queens are on is called the queenside.

On all the boards like this in the book, the pieces are placed as if White started on the bottom two ranks, as shown here.

Who wins?

The winner of the game is the player who can get his pieces into a position where they can trap the enemy king. This is called checkmate. You can find out more about checkmate on page 10.

♛ The queen

On the next few pages you will learn how all the different pieces move. Use your chess set and board to try the moves shown in the pictures.

Each player has one queen. The queen is the most important and valuable piece in your army except for the king.

How the queen moves

The queen can move in any one direction for any number of squares. This makes her a very powerful piece.

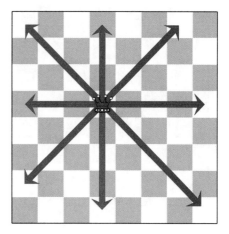

The queen cannot jump over other pieces, though. If a piece from her own army is in the way, the queen cannot go any farther.

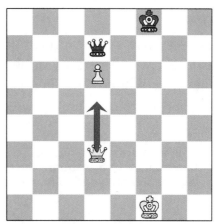

The queen must stop on this square as a pawn is in her way.

If there is an enemy piece in the way, the queen can capture it. You can learn how to capture on the next page.

Capturing

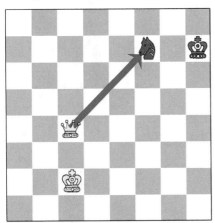

Here the White queen is capturing the Black knight.

To capture an enemy piece you have to land on its square with one of your own pieces.

The Black knight cannot take part in the game any more.

The captured piece is then taken off the board. It cannot be used for the rest of the game.

Taking prisoners

Any one of your pieces can capture any one piece from the other army, as long as it's your turn and you move according to the rules.

Try to capture as many enemy pieces as you can. This will weaken their army and make it easier for you to attack their king.

Puzzles

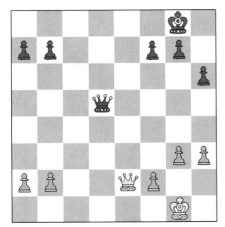

?The Black queen can capture one of the White pawns on her next move. Which one is it?

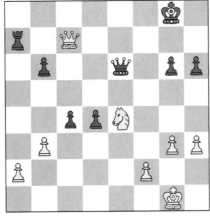

?Which pieces could each queen capture here? Remember how queens move.

Mad queens

The queen was not used in chess until 1475. At first people thought the new game was silly and called it the "mad queen" version. But they soon realized it was a more exciting game.

♟ The pawns

There are eight pawns in each army. They are your least valuable pieces.

How pawns move

Pawns move forward in a straight line, one square at a time.

A pawn's first move is special. For this turn only, you can move it two squares forward if you like.

Diagonal capture

A pawn is the only piece that moves differently when it is **capturing**. It moves one square diagonally forward instead of straight forward.

Here a White pawn captures a Black pawn.

Puzzles

? The White pawn can capture only one of these Black pieces. Which one is it?

? This pawn can capture either of two pieces. Which are they?

Promoting pawns

If one of your pawns reaches the other side of the board, you can change it into any other piece you like, except for the king.

It's usually best to make your pawn a queen, because she is the most powerful piece. You can do this even if your real queen is on the board.

Different styles

In this American chess set, the pieces all look like baseball players. The pawns are the fielders.

Make your pawn look different so that you remember it is now a queen. Here are some suggestions.

If your queen has already been captured, you can put her back on the board instead of the pawn.

If a rook has been captured, you could stand it on its head to represent your new queen.

If a pawn has been taken, put two pawns together on one square, and move them as if they were one piece.

♚ The king

The king is the most important piece in your army. The king can never be taken off the board, but if he is trapped and cannot escape, you lose the game.

The king is the tallest piece in your chess set. He usually has a cross on the top.

Check

If an enemy piece could **capture** your king on its next move, you are in check. The enemy piece is called the checking piece. You must save your king from check right away.

Here the White king is in check. The Black queen could take him on her next move.

How the king moves

The king can move in any direction, but only one square at a time.

Checkmate

If you cannot save your king from check, it is checkmate. This means you have lost the game. The king is never captured, because the game always ends at checkmate.

Three ways to escape from check

1 Move the king out of the way, onto a square where he is no longer in check.

2 Move another piece in the way of the checking piece, to block it.

3 Capture the checking piece with another of your pieces.

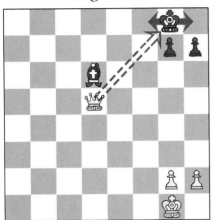

The Black king can move out of check to either of these squares.

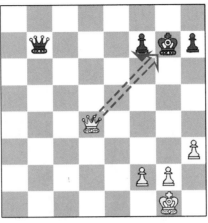

The Black pawn can block the White queen's path, like this.

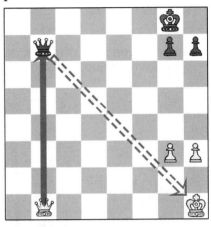

The White queen can capture the Black queen, on her next move.

Watching out for check

Look carefully at all the enemy pieces before you move. Always think about how you can protect your king from danger.

It is against the rules to move your king onto a square where he will be in check. If you do, you must take your turn again.

Puzzle

? The White king is in check from the Black queen. Is it checkmate? Or can White save the king on his next move?

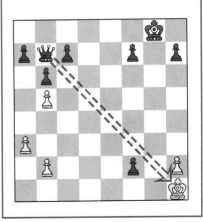

A first game

You can play your first game of chess with just the pawns, the kings and the queens. Read the labels, then set the pieces out correctly on the board.

The pawns are in the rank in front of the queen and king.

The kings and queens stand on the middle squares of the end ranks.

Remember to put the White queen on a pale square.

Rules and tactics

Each player takes a turn moving one piece each. White always starts. This can be helpful, so change armies if you play again. If you touch a piece, you have to move it, so think carefully before you take your turn.

Your goal is to **checkmate** the enemy king. To help do this, try to **capture** your enemy's pieces.

Remember that queens are more valuable than pawns. So don't use your queen to capture a pawn if it will put her at risk.

Quick reminders

1 Pawns move straight forward, one square at a time. On their first move, though, they can move two squares.

2 Pawns capture by moving one square diagonally forward.

3 If a pawn reaches the far side of the board, you can **promote** it.

Find out more: Checkmate - p.10 Capturing - p.7 Promoting pawns - p.9

Make sure there is a white square in the right-hand corner nearest each player.

Remember to put the Black queen on a dark square.

[4] The queen can move in any direction, for as many squares as she likes.

[5] The king can move in any direction, but only one square at a time.

Teamwork

Try to think of your pieces as a team. They can help protect each other if they work together.

If one of your pieces is being attacked, you can

White's king is in check. White moves his pawn to block the check and attack the Black queen.

You can use one piece to "cover" another piece. The covering piece is placed so

The Black king is attacking the White pawn. White moves another pawn to cover it.

block the attack by moving another piece into the way.

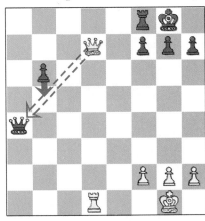

The White queen is attacking the Black queen. A Black pawn blocks the attack.

that if your piece was taken, it could in turn capture the enemy piece.

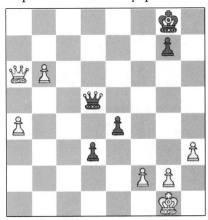

In this game both players have all their remaining pawns covered.

13

♖ The rooks

There are two rooks in each army. Apart from the queens, they are your most valuable pieces.

Rooks are sometimes called castles, because they look like castle towers.

Nobody knows

Nobody is sure where the English word "rook" comes from. Some think it is from an old Persian word "rukh", meaning war chariot. Others think it comes from the Italian word "rocco", which means tower.

How rooks move

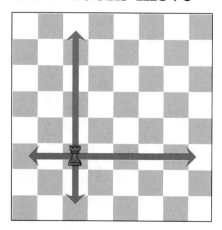

A rook moves in straight lines along the ranks and files. It cannot move diagonally.

A rook can move as many squares as it likes in a straight line, as long as it is not blocked.

A rook can be very powerful. It can control a whole file and a whole rank at the same time.

Protectors

Rooks are good at protecting other pieces. They are very useful for **covering** pawns which are trying to get to the other side of the board to be **promoted**.

If the Black queen captures the advancing pawn, she will be captured by the White rook.

A game with rooks

You can play a game with just the pawns, rooks, king and queen.

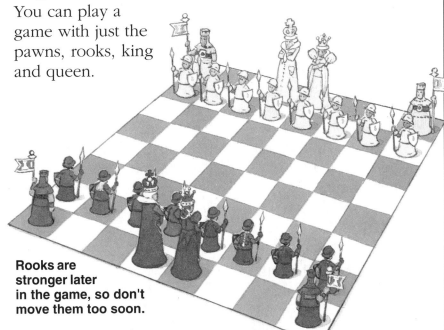

Rooks are stronger later in the game, so don't move them too soon.

Rooks work best in open ranks and files, so when you do move them, don't let them get blocked by other pieces.

Puzzles

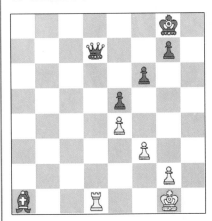

? Which pieces could the White rook **capture** on this board?

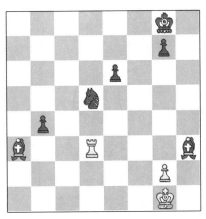

? Can the White rook capture any piece without being taken by a pawn?

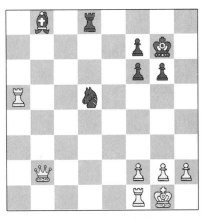

? Which pieces is the Black rook covering in this game?

15

Exchanges

Sometimes you cannot **capture** an enemy piece without losing one of your own. This is called an exchange or a swap. An exchange can be either good, bad or fair, depending on which pieces are swapped and how powerful and valuable they are.

A bad swap

Here the White queen can capture the Black knight, but she would then be captured by a Black pawn. White should not make this swap because he takes a piece worth three points, but loses a piece worth nine.

Points

To help you decide if a swap is good or bad, the pieces are given points. These help you remember how powerful and useful each one is.

 Pawn: 1 point

 Knight*: 3 points

 Bishop*: 3 points

 Rook: 5 points

 Queen: 9 points

 King: 0 points

These points are used only as a guide. There is no scoring in chess.

☹ It is bad swap if you lose a piece that is worth more than the one you take.

If the Black queen (9) takes the White rook (5), she will be taken by the White pawn. This is a bad swap.

☺ It is a good swap if you capture a piece that is more valuable than the one you lose.

If the White pawn (1) takes the Black knight (3), it will be captured by the Black rook. This is a good swap.

☺ It is a fair swap, if you lose a piece of the same value as the one you take.

If the White knight (3) takes the Black bishop (3), it will be taken by the Black pawn. This is a fair swap.

Puzzle

⚬ In each of these games below, a White piece is capturing a Black piece, only to be captured itself. In which game is White making a good swap.

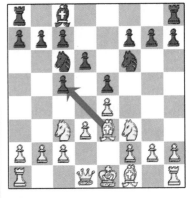

The king has no points. This is because he is never actually captured and so can never be exchanged.

♞ The knights

Each player has two knights. They are the pieces that look like horses. This is because in old-fashioned armies knights were the soldiers that fought on horseback.

How knights move

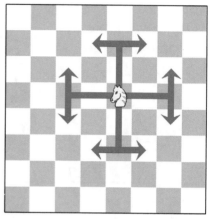

A knight can move in any direction: forward, backward or to the sides. It always moves in an L-shape: two squares in a straight line and then one to the side.

Jumping

The knight is the only piece that can jump over other pieces in its way. Think of a horse jumping and it will help you to remember this.

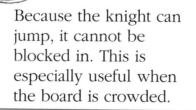

Because the knight can jump, it cannot be blocked in. This is especially useful when the board is crowded.

Even when surrounded by enemy pieces. the knight can jump away.

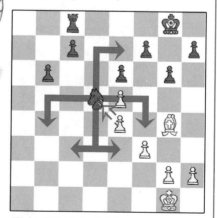

This Black knight can escape from the attacking White pawn onto one of 5 safe squares.

How knights capture and protect

A knight can only **capture** the piece that is on the square it lands on. It cannot capture a piece just by jumping over it.

A knight is strongest in the middle of the board. Here it can **cover** several of your own pieces and attack your enemy's all at the same time.

The Black knight is attacking the White rook and covering the Black bishop and queen.

Early start

Knights are useful at the start of a game. They can jump into the middle of the board even when there are pawns in front of them. It is good to get powerful pieces in the middle early on.

Puzzles

? The White knight can escape capture by moving to only one square. Which square should it move to?

? White's king is in check from Black's queen. In how many ways can the White knight block this check?

Knights of yore

This is a picture of a knight from the oldest complete chess set in the world. It was made nearly 900 years ago. The knight doesn't look very happy does he?

19

♗ The bishops

The two bishops start the game on either side of the king and queen.

How bishops move

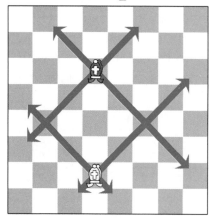

A bishop moves diagonally backward and forward. It can move as many squares at a time as it likes, but it cannot jump over pieces.

Helpful hint

One of the bishops moves diagonally on the dark squares and the other on the light squares.

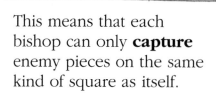

This means that each bishop can only **capture** enemy pieces on the same kind of square as itself.

Capturing trick

If you have the chance, position a bishop so that it is attacking two enemy pieces at the same time. This is called a fork.

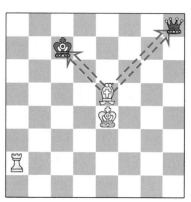

The White bishop is attacking the Black king and queen. Black must move her king and lose her queen.

Find out more: Capturing - p.7

Puzzles

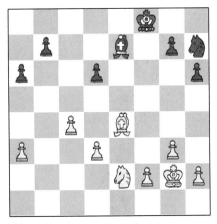

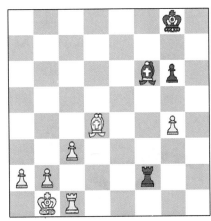

? Can the White bishop capture any of the pieces on this board?

? On this board, which bishop, Black or White, is attacking in a fork?

? White's bishop has the rook and knight in a fork. What's Black's best move?

Into battle

Now you can try a game using all your pieces. Plan ahead as much as possible, but don't make a final decision on what to move before it is your turn. Your opponent's move may change your mind.

Look at all the pieces on the board. Then ask yourself four questions:

1 Are all my pieces defended, especially the king?

2 Can any of my pieces be captured?

3 Can I capture an enemy piece, and will it be safe if I do?

4 Can I figure out what the other player is planning?

You are a little like a general directing your troops.

Elephants on the chess board

Old Indian chess sets used elephants, instead of bishops. Bishops were introduced in Europe in the Middle Ages when the Church was very powerful.

Special moves

Here are two special moves you can use to help protect your own pieces and attack your opponents'.

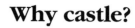

Castling

This is a move for the king and one rook. It is the only time you can move two pieces in one turn.

Why castle?

After castling, the king is tucked away in a corner, so he is easier to protect. But the rook has more space, so it can attack more easily. It is most useful to castle early in the game.

To castle on the **kingside**, move the king two squares toward the rook, and the rook moves two squares the other way.

To castle on the **queenside**, move the king two squares toward the rook, and the rook three squares the other way.

Castling is the only time the king can move two squares at once. After you have castled, the king and the rook always end up next to each other.

Fair play

There is a special organization called the World Chess Federation which makes sure that everyone plays by the same rules.

Puzzle

? Can Black or White castle in this game? If so, on which side (kingside or queenside)? Use the checklist on page 23.

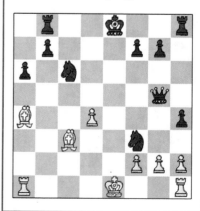

Find out more: Kingside - p.5 Queenside - p.5 Check - p.10 Capturing - p.7

Castling checklist

There are four things you need to check before you castle:

CHECKLIST
1, No pieces in the way.
2, First move.
3, Not in check before / after

1 There must be no pieces in the way between the king and the rook.

2 It must be the very first move of the game for both pieces.

Neither army can castle because there are pieces between each king and rook.

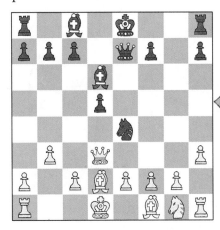

Here Black can castle on the kingside. White has already moved his king so cannot.

3 The king must not be in **check** before or after you castle.

4 The king must not be in check in the square he passes through.

Black cannot castle here because her king is in check from the White bishop.

White cannot castle as his king would be in check from the Black bishop during the move.

En passant

En passant (say on passon) means "in passing". It is a special move using a pawn.

After a pawn has moved two squares as its first move, an enemy pawn can **capture** it as if it had moved only one.

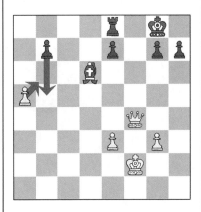

The White pawn can now capture the Black pawn using the en passant rule.

Opening moves and tricks

The first moves you make in a game are very important. They can put you in a weak or a strong position for the rest of the game.

Pawns first

You could move the two middle pawns as your first two turns. This helps you control the middle of the board. It also clears the way for the bishops.

The most useful pieces early in a game are usually the pawns, bishops and knights.

If you use the queen too early in the game you might put her in danger.

Moving a side pawn is not as useful. It doesn't help you control the middle and traps stronger pieces on the back rank.

The rooks are more useful later when there are fewer pieces left on the board.

Look after the king carefully right from the beginning.

White has not made a good start here, but Black has, clearing the way for her bishops.

Next moves

After the pawns, move your bishops and knights. They are much stronger in the middle of the board. When you have done this, you can **castle**. This protects your king behind a row of pawns.

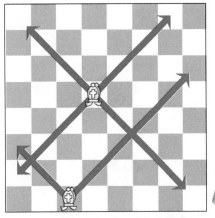

At the edge of the board, bishops can move to only 7 squares. In the middle, they can move to 13.

Grains of truth

There are more possible games of chess than there are grains of sand in the whole world.

Capturing tricks

Once you have pieces in the middle of the board, try some tricks to help **capture** enemy pieces.

One trick is a **fork.** One piece attacks two enemy pieces at the same time.

A skewer forces a valuable piece to move so a less valuable piece is captured.

A pin is an attack on a piece which is protecting a piece more valuable than itself.

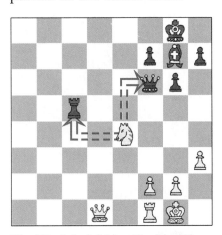

The Black knight is attacking the queen and the rook. If either piece moves, the other will be captured.

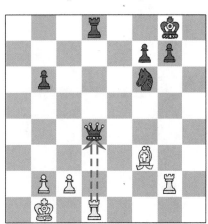

White's rook is attacking Black's queen. The queen must move, so the Black rook is captured.

Black's knight can't escape from White's attack because this would put the Black queen at risk.

Writing chess down

There is a code for writing down chess moves, called notation. Once you can read it, you can follow games in books and magazines. This is very good practice.

Most people use algebraic notation. It uses letters and numbers for the pieces and the squares on the board.

The letters and numbers are plotted as if you are playing as White, so the board looks like this.

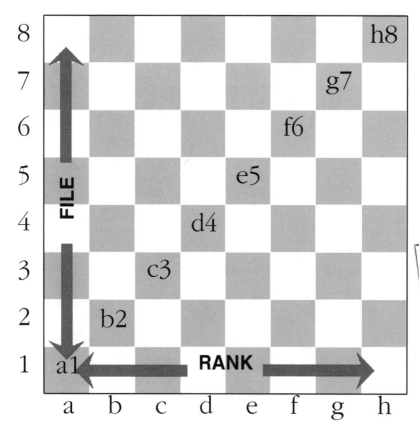

A helpful hint

Put a large piece of paper under your chess board, and write the letters and numbers around the edge.

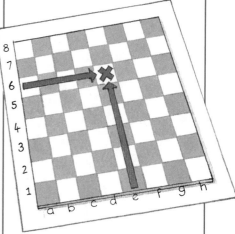

To find square e6, follow file e and rank 6. The square where they meet is e6.

Each rank has a number, starting with the rank closest to White. Each file is given a small letter, starting with the file on White's left. Each square on the board is identified by the letter of the file it is in, and the number of the rank it is in.

Pieces and moves

The pieces are coded as capital letters, except for the pawn which has no symbol. To write down a move, you put the letter of the piece, then the letter and number of the square it moves to. For a pawn, just write the letter and number of the square it moves to.

King is K

Rook is R

Bishop is B

Queen is Q

Pawn has no letter

Knight is N

Making it clear

It may not always be clear which piece is moving, so sometimes the file or rank that a piece is on is given too, to help identify it.

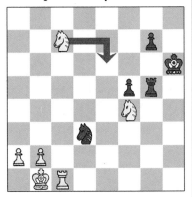

The move Ne6 could be made by both White knights. Nce6 tells you it is the kinght on the c-file that is moving.

Puzzle

? How would you write down the move on this board, using notation?

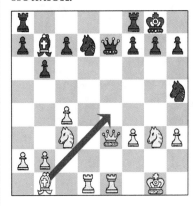

This move is Ne4.

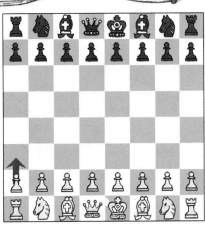

This move is a3.

White first

When a game is written up, the moves are numbered. White's moves are written first. So **1.e3, Nf6** means on their first moves, White moved a pawn to e3 and Black moved a knight to f6.

If Black's move is written without White's, dots are printed after the move number. So **8...Kd6** means for her eighth move Black moved her king to d6.

Capturing

When one piece **captures** another, write the letter for the piece (unless the capturing piece is a pawn), then **x**, and then the letter and number of the square it moves to.

The White rook capturing the Bishop is written Rxc6.

Check and checkmate

If a move gives **check**, a plus sign like this **+** is written after it.

This move is Re7+.

If a move gives **checkmate**, two plus signs are written after it.

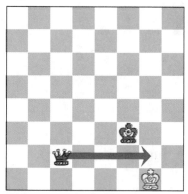

This move is Qg2++.

Castling

If you **castle** on the **kingside**, you write down 0-0.

If you castle on the **queenside**, you write down 0-0-0.

The end of a game

In the shortest game of chess, Black can checkmate White in only two moves.

But many games go on until hardly any pieces are left on the board at all.

Puzzle

☐ White is in trouble. Can he avoid losing by forcing a draw?

1.f3, e5; 2.g4, Qh4++

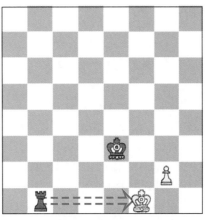

Black's rook checkmates White.

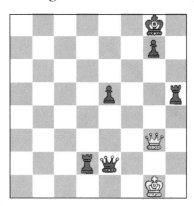

Drawn games

A game is drawn if no player can give checkmate. There are two main sorts of draw: stalemate and perpetual check.

Stalemate is when a player isn't in check, but cannot make any move that is allowed.

In perpetual check, one player keeps putting the other in check, but can never acheive checkmate.

If this is repeated three times, the game ends in a draw.

It is White's turn to move, but the only moves he can make would put his king in check.

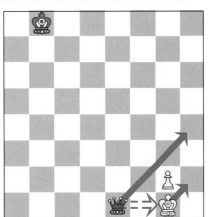

White moves Kh2 to escape check. Black moves Qh4+, putting White in check again.

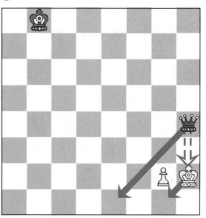

White has to move back to g1 where Black can put him in check once more.

Puzzle answers

The queen - p.7

The pawns - p.8

p.8 continued

The White pawn could capture either the Black knight or the Black bishop.

The king - p.11

It is checkmate.
The king cannot move onto a safe square. (If he moves one square to the left, he is in check from the Black pawn, if he moves diagonally forward, he is still in check from the Black queen.) There is no White piece which can block the check, and the Black queen cannot be captured.

The rooks - p.15

The White rook could capture either the Black queen or the Black bishop.

Yes. The White rook can capture the Black bishop to its right, without being taken by a Black pawn.

The Black rook is covering the bishop, which is under attack from the White queen, and the knight which is under attack from the White rook.

Exchanges - p.17

White is making a good swap in the top game, where he is capturing a queen (9 points) and losing a rook (5 points). In the bottom game, White is making a bad swap. He is capturing a pawn (1 point) but losing a bishop (3 points).

The knights - p.19

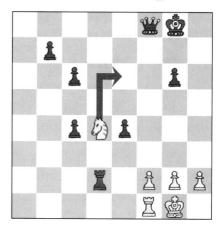

White's knight can block check in two ways:

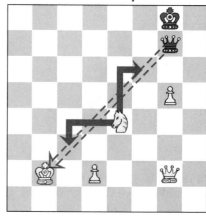

The bishops - p.21

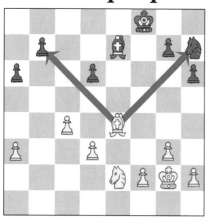

The White bishop is attacking in a fork.

If the Black rook moves to the left-hand corner of the board, it escapes being captured and covers the attacked Black knight:

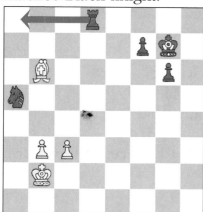

Special moves - p.22

White cannot castle on either side because his king is in check from the Black knight. Black can castle on the kingside, but not on the queenside where the rook has already moved.

Writing chess down - p.27

This move is written as Be4.

The end of a game - p. 29

If White's queen was off the board, the game would end in stalemate. (The White king could not move without putting himself in check). Therefore, in order to get a draw, White has to force Black to capture his queen.

White's queen moves to g7 and captures Black's pawn. This puts the Black king in check. To escape check the Black king has to capture the queen.

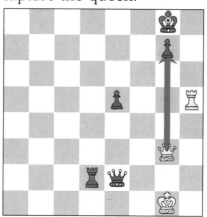

Useful addresses

United States Chess Federation
186 Route 9 West
New Windsor
NY 11553
USA

The Chess Federation of Canada
2212 Gladwin Crescent E-1
Ottawa
Ontario K1B 5N1
Canada

New Zealand Chess Federation
P.O. Box 3130
Wellington
New Zealand

British Chess Federation
9A Grand Parade
St Leonard's on Sea
East Sussex
TN38 0DD

Index

ISBN 0-590-67312-2

Copyright © 1995 by Usborne Publishing Ltd. First published in Great Britain in 1995 by Usborne Publishing Ltd. All rights reserved. Published by Scholastic Inc., 555 Broadway, New York, NY 10012, by arrangement with Usborne Publishing Ltd.

12 11 10 9 8 7 6 5 4 3 2   6 7 8 9/9 0 1/0

Printed in the U.S.A.   09

First Scholastic printing, January 1996